# A CALL FROM THE HEART

A CALL FROM THE HEART

AF578614

JASKIRAN KOUR
@STARBOXER

Copyright © Jaskiran Kour,@starboxer
All Rights Reserved.

This book has been self-published with all reasonable efforts taken to make the material error-free by the author. No part of this book shall be used, reproduced in any manner whatsoever without written permission from the author, except in the case of brief quotations embodied in critical articles and reviews.

The Author of this book is solely responsible and liable for its content including but not limited to the views, representations, descriptions, statements, information, opinions and references ["Content"]. The Content of this book shall not constitute or be construed or deemed to reflect the opinion or expression of the Publisher or Editor. Neither the Publisher nor Editor endorse or approve the Content of this book or guarantee the reliability, accuracy or completeness of the Content published herein and do not make any representations or warranties of any kind, express or implied, including but not limited to the implied warranties of merchantability, fitness for a particular purpose. The Publisher and Editor shall not be liable whatsoever for any errors, omissions, whether such errors or omissions result from negligence, accident, or any other cause or claims for loss or damages of any kind, including without limitation, indirect or consequential loss or damage arising out of use, inability to use, or about the reliability, accuracy or sufficiency of the information contained in this book.

Made with ♥ on the Notion Press Platform
www.notionpress.com

I kept you as a hidden secret , which is open to all in the form of poetry . This book is dedicated to ones who were really failed to mailed the heartfelt messages to their beloved from the mouth . From where should I learnt the languages , to make you feel , What ? I feel for you .

*"Miracles happens , the time I pen down you*

*each word become wild and starts dancing on the paper heart .*

*_@starboxer"*

# Contents

# Contents

# Preface

***"YOU are the wound , I never want to heal***

***And the most beautiful accident , I had ever met ".***

*_@starboxer* "

I 'll write you in such a way that one who reads you (will get a fragrance in my words at the time of imagining you ).

# Prologue

If you have a dreamboat , my writings will help you to convey the sugar messages to your beloved .

And if you have not any , I'll make you helpless to find a connection after reading my book .

# Acknowledgements

***I consider you , above all in humans , a heartfelt thanks to (my fragrance) who flows in the air , I breathe . And I can't afford you but I can carry you secretly in the veins in the form of pure blood . Here , I convert you in the forms of poetry , listen to the call from my heart .***

*_@starboxer* ”

I owe my gratitude to all my friends who were always ready to back up me when i really felt myself in problem ( my crime partners ) you all pull me back from the puzzled situations .

dear reader , read my talks of heart (poems ) through the signals of emotions and make them error free .

# Poetry Last Breath

You met , when I was in the critical phase as in ICU
of my life - messily roaming here and there .
Even , struggling hard to breathe .
Ahhhhh! Then , I found you
The only aid " as my last breath " , who makes me alive .
If I had to sell -
The very last piece of my flesh , from the body
The cost to gain you , whole gladly I 'll do ......
Think??? That much imprint you left in my heart .
Despite of all , I felt restless
when I found no pieces of you near me .
Isn't you , exactly reassembles
The carbon copy of my dream soulmate ;
The soul , I wished for .

# Poetry Foolish Heart

You broke promises
Still I trust you And cause my friend.
Many times, I thought it
Not to truest you.
Still it get lost when I see you.
Time and again heart says
Not it make you my close one.
Your"s fan queue is very long
But I"m at theend
To lose you"Ifear a lot.
With me . You won;t come
But thisfoolishheart don't understand
Make me crazy your words.
Anyone otherthan you, I don't see
I'm devastated fully;
Here nothing you cost.
D0n't go ,I need you
Give me ; a reason of doing this
Leaving all like this .don't go.

# Poetry The Disciple

Don't ask, to reside in your breath
    Fix me, like a dust in your footwear.
    Like a friend , the name ofyour's
    I used to chant , to meditate.
    Gladly die for you, if I supposed to
    Have place in your feet; stroke of luck.
    Shatter my dreams, neglect my eagerness
    Put me off, its your wish
    Do a favour name me once.
    Elegant air, the heaven's path
    Ended up all here, you are my God.
    You reside in my mind, Oh! mentor
    Fallen foryou, since I met you
    All because of your's kind prespective.

# Poetry Wake Up Call !

Dear , Moon ! I'm in love with a distant star
Did you know where it had gone ?
There is a huge rush
In the pulses of heart
As if my star , Is not well ?
The eyes of mine , gets sick off
Cause my star , Hadn't give me a look for so long .
Obfuscating thoughts , Tangled
The signals of my mind -
And alert me about your new match .
Do prove wrong , the indications
Of your new longings ;
As, after you , Nothing I had .
Earlier , I'm suffering with plague
Don't do bluff me .
After you , I 'll remain as a dead soul .
Remember ! A slit in our bond
Will never be fulfilled by the
- tears of your regret -

# Poetry Thumping Heart

Somewhere miles away , When
I breathe fragnance of you ;
A little louder my heart starts thump - thump .
Thumping of heart , From so far
Defines the connectivity of a single soul
Lie into two different bodies .
Darling ! The intangible moments of love
We live together ; Is anchored deep into
The weiis of my heart .
My love , has no vaildation
Cause I went ; If it's real
Surely , You'll sense and feel it .
Everything is lovelable of you
Apart from your absence,
Hence

# Poetry Melt Into You

When I look into candy purple eyes
I go deep inside you , I started
Melting into you .
I drown so deep into you
That I got tangled into -
The signals of nerves of brain .
The way you treats me
( A special warmth of priority you gave )
Forms a soft corner of you .
All is you , have a home in me
Is judged by your aroma , people sensed
When I pen down you in my poetry .
The strings of your heart
Leads to a path called love ;
Which defines the authentication of us , as lovers .

# Poetry Branches Of Soul

You spread
Into every branches of
my soul .
You flow like the oxygen
Which help my heart to pump out
And cause me to function into real .
Every motion , I perform
Is run by the accessibility of you .
As I permit you , To reside in me .
I can bear anything
Except , the one from your falsity .
Destiny adjoins us for a reason
Do prove everyone , You can stick
For me forever .

# Poetry Burning Bed

All night ! I roited with nights
thinking about you ? How you dissolve
into other ? How they surprise you ?
With a glass of sherry
In your hand , you enjoy the date .
O, darling . How wisely you forget me ?
Lend me to path , Where ?
May be , I'm able to disappear myself
In order to burnt myself and turn into ashes .
I worried about you : Onto the burning bed
Every night , While recalling the vows .
Had it not ? So far you had gone
Memories couldn't allow me to get off from you ;
In such a way , I mesmerized in you .
Come back , Only if to heal me
Pour life into a black dead soul .

# Poetry A Heartless Person

Fell in love , With a heartless person
And it forced , cry in secret .
You left me , Stay with someone else
Well, You are happy , but I don't think ?
Heard many times , false promises
Why ? You , return gifts I gave ,

Leaving me , Will be easier
Listen! I'm not felling for you .
Still , I remember you
Many other came after you .
I carries the cementeries
Beneath my skin - The only reason not to hook up .
Just sorry !Don't want the bond we had.
Forever are the memories , Not the people
Trust me ! A new bond will bliss your heart .
Don't want much , Just your time
Admire my feelings , Only want you not new .

# Poetry Pause

Expectations the heaviest weightage
And like venom slowly first ;
It flows into my bloodstream .
Then it enters into my heart
Hence disturbing the signals of love
Resulting in making my soul deep black .
I tied my heart with yours
Although after departure , All I found it as a broken window ;
Which chooses to close the door for the new longings.
To make you known , the fact -
Yes , I do yearn , crave for you
But I never had you , my incomplete wish .
The time conspire and makes me fool
Cause still I pause , Each time
Whenever I found pieces of you , near me .

# Poetry Without A Doubt

Darling , It makes no odd , what if ?
I choose you and And I kept choosing you
Without a doubt ,
The allegations people put , The certification they claim
The flaws inside you , Didn't
Stop me to love you ; Without a doubt
I choose you , And I'll choose you .
Either you treat me cold
Or hold and hug me tightly .
I'll choose you , Without a doubt .
No matter , How much hurdles
I ought to face like thorns , In order to
Have a beautiful flower like you ;
I'll choose you , Without a doubt
I drenched in blissfulness , knows nothing
I high in ecstasy in love , choose you .
In such a way , I dissolve into you .

# Poetry Imprints On Hearts

Imprints on my heart, the name of yours
Oh! darling I got a identity by you.
Ishh! By making me your first and foremost priority
You made yourself, stitched with me.
Signals get burst, from the veins
Of my heart and mind, calling you again and again.
Facial expressions; works as a display screen
For the way, you feel when I hold you.
Although, I die; the time you'll disappear
Cause no parts of me wants to apart from you
A short message! Intervals ruins the relations
No matter, How beateous the season of love was.

# Poetry At Comfort

Normal self is pure
Than the purest pearls
Feeling jealous from you, the angles.
At comfort,
My eyes are always -
Never gets, enough of you.
Even God, is in the awe of beauty
Her praise, is in the words of flowers.
You've got millions of trillon's fans
While nobody chooses me.
To look at your's face,
Early in the morning -
Only thought came across my mind.

# Poetry Eraser

Devastated me, In a facinated way
Wins a loosing heart, What a play!
Erase the happiness, my living root
Cause all you wanna, make me mute
Filled my eyes, with acqua blue
Haunting teeth, Cause my brain chew
Fluctuating happiness, An immense guilt
Showering blessing of , Curse and spilt.
Warmth ofsadness, Make me joy
Yourannoying words, All i enjoy.
A straight word, Mystery only i have
Confess thebitterness, Insert in heart cave
Bertrayed me , with habitus words
Fud the toxins, To the bird of heart
Screaming for breathe, Lost in you
Unshed life, Cause it flew.
Weeks and months, filtration starts
Smile gets filtered, Purified the heart
Turns allow me, Into loneliness
Show pure magic of, Love and witness
Console me , With thorny bushes arms
After a long , find relief in harm .
Appericiable wounds of respect , All I gain
Travel in train of love , Presented me pain .
Erase our memories , a big salute
Cause all you want , make me mute .

# Sugar Talks

Some people are unpaid like ( my fragrance ) they come , they make you smile , irritate you

and can convert the hell into heaven only . Aaawwwww! I don't valve you but its true that you

are like the oxygen , my everything .

"*In order to keep you , I can even erase myself.*

*_@starboxer* "

# Poetry Puzzleboard

In a puzzleboard,
We are framed
Timely tested, in numerous forms.
Shuffled by different obstacles
Of people; love seasons.
Bodily partner of both, has been changed
But no new body get fit into this
- Puzzleboard -
Although! Our magnetic heart knows
Where to repel or attract.
Facing all the hurdles, You and I
Solve the puzzle, full of doubtful tasks
And converted into an answer key
- as lovers -

# Sugar Talks

Honey , You are the fullstop of my heart . As I don't want to see a view accept you .
The eyes of mine always search you in the blur vision and my heart miss you in
the presence
of the crowd of people . My heart stop searching for anything , unless
- I found you -

*"my love for you is like counting the raindrops*
*_@starboxer"*

# Poetry Close To The Grave

Close to the grave , I wish
I could found you , Near my dead body
As close as , The icarus to the moon .
Hey! Don't be sad , I'll
No more irritate you , with my stupid writings .
Just enjoy ! I am dead now .
Darling! The unsend messages
Are burried with me , in my heart .
Alas ! Can't able to define my longings .
Entire life , I spend with the memories
Which moments creates with you .
Actually I live each seconds of time ,
That's a matter of couple of time , Just make it
Come to my graveyard ,Have a look on me .
That look of your's , Free my soul from the universe .
Then , nobody will disturb you
From the boring poems for sure
And you'll be free , free , just free from me .
Close to the Grave , I wish
I would dream , a dream , To see you next to me
To celebrate , And laugh at the current situation .

# Poetry Digestible For You

Just like -

A lemon juice , I'm
Digestible and detoxic for you .
Consume me , I'll make you
Fit to run into the false world .
Boom! I soaked myself into your soul
The hours of the clock , Whole 24'
Knocks towards you , all the time .
Honey, I miss you and every breath ,
I breathe reminds me meeting you again .

# Poetry Parcel

Honey ! pick me up
Cause am your parcel ;
God has dispatched me at your address .
A parcel contains a heart
Which stays mad in the fondness of you .
A destiny , I ( the parcel) knows
To reach where , is You .
Open me , I may surprise you
With the longings ; Emotions
Engulf with in me , from the old time .
Ishhhhh! I lost completely in you .
Each brick of my body is -
Cemented by the fragrance of you .
As a whole ,You pierced
- Into my soul -
Accept or readdress me ,
But I 've a permanent address that's you ;
As I am meant to find you .

# Sugar Talks

No care ,

no tears ,no fear to lose you,

no more heart talks ,

no more night calls .

You through everything in dustbin , even me .

everthing is wastage the talks , after listening to it ; it burns my soul

and the stink heart release kills the fragrance . The signals of seperation I ignore ,

now I will follow ..... I think it's the hunger call of soul , but you shut the door of heart ,

so I step out from you .

Don't you say , you hurt me or miss me ( cause you are the only reason for not being us together )

"*Steadily ,the fear of losing you* "

Shakes my soul , like the hurricane

_@starboxer

""

# Poetry Tangled Me

The silence in you , beauty in words
Everything of you , Tangled me .
By capturing your gait styles
Peacock itself , Become the world popular.
In ocean , When you look
Even the thrilling waves , calms down .
In hotter summer , The sweat of your's
Turn desolate land , Into a greenry one .
The soil , becomes pretentious
When your feet , touches ground .
I remember everything , Hadn't forget anything .
Chameleons halt , changing color
Become stir , When they see you .
When sweltering heat , Reaches you
The icy clouds , starts raining ;
This thing of yours , Tangled me .
When your eyes , opens
The bleak Universe , Turns into colored one .
Whether you kept me , In feet
Or compare in , With ashes ;
Accept my fan proposal .
Losing thought of you , I kept
In the bars of mind -
The curiosity for you , Tangled me .

# Poetry Lavender Dream

Impulsiveness in the beat , A huge rush in the signals of heart
Parellel to my heart , When my retina get filtered ;
I saw my dreamboat , Ishhhhh! In my lavender dream .
A vissage ; With brown silky hairs
Dark deep cyan eyes , Keep on fathoming the ocean of love .
In my unsound heart , Which pauses it beat .
Everything here blur , Brain starts stammering
Thoughts if were roiting in between ; Pulse beat raise as an athlete one .
For my solace , I anchored the time .
In Zeppelin , Where two pairs of eyes converted into one
Our breath freeze for a moment , Then the lavender dream open up into real .
Forever is a lie , You last as a memory .
Why so scurry ? Don't be so tyrannical ?
Don't seed a thistle in my heart ? I asked
Lol ! A tragedy happened , As the eyes gets open .

# Sugar Talks

The absence of yours , dims the light of passing the signals of happiness , although

worsening the strength and decay the flower of heart . Don't know when the so called right time

comes , when I found you sitting near by me . Till then , I satisfy myself each day of every year by meeting

you in my home palace called dream .

*"I write about you , in different flavours to make you fall in love .*

*_@starboxer "*

# Poetry Farewell Of Love

Lo ! Time comes of departure
All left behind , Epoch of departue
Forever is a lie , You , turn as a question mark ?
A sudden attack , Unsound my heart ;
On it's left side - Only memories
And at the right - its a broken window .
The view of proposal , Blocked for new match
Still reserved for you, Cause of your aroma in me ;
Lets ! cheers to the beautiful moments of past that's (You )
Being a presumptuous , I 'll remember you
Will allow you to enter , In my dreams
You are a sojourner , Still I accept you .
Darling , Its you , Who yearn and search
For someone to care for , but
For me , You 'll be the fullstop .
You make me fimilar , With the season of love
Filled the calender , Of journey with memories .
(Enjoyed the togtherness , What a bliss ? )
Emotions of love ? What a sheer bunkum ?
R.I.P ! here my feelings for you , In a ditch .
Farewell of love , Is quite feasible
To bid you a farewell , Here 's a candle
Light it , In remembrance of cold love -
Reminder , No new still you .

# Poetry Invisible Tears

As a gift of loyality , The Invisible tears
Roll on , Each time when my heart ache for you .
What's the matter ? What's my mistake .
Tell me once , we 'll figure it out .
Invisible tears , Are more dangerous
More powerful , Then the spoken words .
Disconnection from you , cuts and break me
Into several pieces , Like a butcher do .
Hence , making my mind senseless , my heart beatless
And Although me , a alive dead body .
People love , But I really hate to
----Write you like this ----
You , left me awake all night
And as a result , I started writing ;
I turned my invisible tears into poetry .
Loads of love , To your personal profession
Of yearn and crave , With the new ones .

## Sugar Talks

“ *If you choose me , I 'll never make you feel regret for me*
*_@ starboxer* ”

in all the seasons of love , I’ll be your raincoat protecting you from all the odds . I ’ll be there with you under the sky , counting the stars and making you smile .

# Poetry Poetic Penance

Loving you , Turns into testimony of loyality
Cause after you , Everything sounds hell to me .
Caring you , rewards me a wound
Where I lost myself , In order to heal you .
Noticing you , turns into imprisionment of beautiful view
As my eyes blur everything , like you the end .
Thinking you , Tangled my subconscious memeory
You are the only thought , stuck into my mind .
Loving you , make a fullstop for new episode
Cause memory , dislike to forget you .
Writting you , Is a poetic penance
Words didn't allow me , to describe anyone else .

# Poetry Sugarcoated Talks

Little by Little
You filled me
With your sugarcoated talks .
The aroma of you
Was smell deeply in me ;
Whenever I shutdown
The window of my eyes .
Ishhhh! The look of yours
Was enough to conquer my heart .
A secret , the hidden mystery
Love you to the square of infinity .
Honey , You 'll be the end picture
My eyes wants to capture before death ,
Cause you would lie into my soul forever .

## Sugar Talks

On hearing , You , as a blessing , it felt like the big boulders and stones of my heart starting melting ,
that much comfort you gave . Your talks , are a piece of art and excitement which guides me how to face
numerous onslanghts of time . Thanks to God ! for showering the sweet water and grace ( in the desert of my life ) in the form of you .

*"In the core of memory , I consider you as my favourite emotion.*
*_ @starboxer "*

# Poetry Injecting Poison

Honey , I deal with you perfectly
knowing your flaws , errors
All I catch your teething nerve.
Slowly and slowly
I inject poison in your love,
Very smartly , very smoothly .
Within couple of times ,
When I catch you near me ,
I took the decision to detach you .
In order , by not letting you
Into my nerves , I protect you
From being the original you .
I save you
From your identity being lost
If you lost in me , You 'll disappear .
All I done , Cause I
Am a fragile connection for a perfect bond
And if I had a future , I might spoil you .

# Sugar Talks

Secretly , O secretly ! You divert from the bond , it hurts but nothig is going on my way .

If anything was piercing me through , was your absence. Although , the memories we create are enough

to memorize you ages by ages .

"*Blood runs so fast , into the veins ;*

*Thinking about why your behaviour has changed .*

"

# Poetry Length X Breadth

You extended upto
The length and breadth of
'My soul ' .
My brain stammers
The signals get puzzled
What to say ? How to treat you ?
At my hard , I fail to connect , What to choose ?
All the directions , seems miserable ,
Although my compass stops and find you ;
The only destiny - I'm roaming around .
Lol ! I pick a flower ,
In order to warm meeting you , but
Lost in the fragrance of you .
Then , When I get back my conscious
I found , very few pieces of you near me
As you had gone .
With a sudden pinch , In my unsound heart
I bid you a bye , but my eyes haven't .

# Poetry In Love

Considering no one is there ,
Like beloved , pursuing you everywhere .
Why ? We dares to lose
Why ? Finding arduous like-wise to choose .
Why ? It happens , i used to care
Why? when anyone see beloved , I can't bear
Why? we can't see in beloved eyes
Why ? By seeing our heart pulse rise .
Why ? can't see beloved see in distress
Why ? while seeing , We 're in stress
Why ? When you cry my heart burst out .
Why ? Always ready to quarrel
Without knowing the outcomes.

# Poetry Route

Inhaling the same 0xygen in
Still we are too for
Why our route are aparted?
Come under one shelter;
Of heart to live in , so
Why our route are apparted ?
Oh! lover .We have alike features:
of humanus "A soul, a heart"- so
Why our route are aparted ?
You picked peace over drama
And love over the flows.
I love every brick of your soul, Darling.
Little effort of yours
Can make you mine forever
All I have is one route that's you.

# Sugar Talks

"*Lies all around , especially the promises.*

*_@starboxer*"

Afresh bond, temporary relief after then the heart roars , causes the pain # shit to attachment ,

nobody can glue the broken pieces of heart not even the butterflies we felt earlier .

When I need you hear me out , you shuts down the windows of ear and become

dead (acts like a dumb )

# Poetry Spec Of Dust

Keep me in contact of you, All the time
Accept me in the form of spec of dust
Under your feet .
Like water , I can immerse in you
Cause all I 'm yours , You 're not mine .
Although , allow me to be a -apart of you
From being so long , I 'm your oldest darling !
Being a spec of dust , I gave my control
Upto you , take me where you want to be ?
Kill me or hate me
Don't do apart me .
Leave it dear! I'll never leave you
Don't take tension , I'll do as you say .
What I have, none have in this world
My wanting is divine for you .

# Sugar Talks

I don't know where to go in order to search you or you can say to heal me .

I constantly wander here and there to get a smell of you .

And news about you makes me alive , the way you answer the puzzleboard of my life is really unforgetable .

> *"Calenders of Calendars , passed away*
> *Still I'm in fond of you.*
> *_@starboxer"*

# Poetry Dislocate

Every minute , Every hour
Each time , Each wine
I yearn you , like a hell !
Eyes become wild red in pain
As they stuck at the route , Where you left ;
Make them in relief , Come back !
After departure , I felt like -
You dislocate each bone of my body
And make me body left , in severe pain .
Thinking about you
Whole brutally , I missed you in day
And all night , I spent awake
Roited at the burning bed .
A sudden change in your behaviour
Discomfort me from you
And as a result I detach you .

# Poetry Unsend Messages

Unsend messages , Of love
I used to write , And then erase it
Which I wanted to confess ; Left unsend
Cause I 'm afraid to lose you .
Why I care ? Why I search you ?
All the rarebit feelings , I want to express .
Somehow I feel shy , to describe it .
You , are the reason I smile , I cry
I had gain my lost smile , And started to laugh louder
Whenever my mood swings , I yearn you
Wanted to burst out, the mixture of feelings , I had .
You are the wound , I never want to heal
And the most beautiful accident , I had ever met .
Accounts of messages , Are being reserved
Only for you , because you study me all .

# Sugar Talks

You will be shined in the words of my talks as a majestic blessing . Tell me ? who doesn't wants to be happy , everyone is trying very hard in their prayers in order to have you . Boom! How lucky I'm, cause

I know you are already mine .

*"The one who will read my poems , will beome insane while searching you .*
*_@starboxer .* "

***Eyes on you , no new , still you .***

*_@starboxer*"

# Fragrance

*"You , open the doors of sorrows*
*And step aside my unstitch heart*
*In-order to feel the fractures , to heal me .*
*You deserve , I kept you " above all " .*
*_@starboxer .* "

I carry you , under the cemeteries of my skin as a fragrance .

www.ingramcontent.com/pod-product-compliance
Lightning Source LLC
LaVergne TN
LVHW041127150826
845673LV00007B/2212

* 9 7 9 8 8 9 5 8 8 7 0 9 7 *